101 more conversation starters for couples

101 more conversation starters for couples

GARY CHAPMAN

& RAMON PRESSON

Northfield Publishing
CHICAGO

ISBN: 978-0-8024-0838-9

We hope you enjoy this book from Northfield Publishing.
Our goal is to provide high-quality, thought-provoking books
and products that connect truth to your real needs and challenges.
For more information on other books and products written
and produced from a biblical perspective, go to
www.moodypublishers.com or write to:

Northfield Publishing
820 N. LaSalle Boulevard
Chicago, IL 60610

1 3 5 7 9 10 8 6 4 2

Printed in the United States of America

Tips for Using 101 More Conversation Starters

Your spouse is a fascinating person, a treasure trove of meaningful, humorous, and profound experiences, thoughts, feelings, ideas, memories, hopes, dreams, beliefs, and convictions. These questions celebrate the depth and wonderful mystery of your mate. Questions invite disclosure, and disclosure launches discovery. Discovery enriches a marriage and builds intimacy. Use the following 101 questions to prompt meaningful, in-depth discussions and to affirm and encourage your spouse.

Here are some ways to use the questions:

- During dinner at home (if you don't have children)
- During a quiet moment in the evening
- At bedtime (if both of you are alert)
- During dinner on a date night
- While in the car during a long drive

While the easiest way to proceed through the questions is to use them in the order they are presented, another possibility is that your spouse and you take turns in selecting the questions. We recommend that you do only one or two questions at a time. These questions are like dessert—a small and satisfying portion creates the anticipation for more later. *101 More Conversation Starters for Couples* offers a process to enjoy, not a project to complete.

Have fun with these questions two or three times each week and watch intimacy grow in your marriage.

What was something that you really wanted to do but were not allowed to do as a child or teen?

more conversation starters for couples

What is one of the best/worst customer service experiences you've had?

question
2
more conversation starters for couples

What is one saying, quote,
or Bible verse that you
strongly identify with?

The airline overbooked our flight and we voluntarily gave up our seats in exchange for two round-trip tickets to any destination in the United States, excluding Hawaii and Alaska. Where do you want to go, and what time of year?

question

4

more conversation starters for couples

In Joshua 13:1 God tells Joshua that in spite of his advanced years there is still much land to be conquered. Do you have some "land" you still want to "conquer," something you want to accomplish?

Recall something you experienced

or a place you visited that

didn't live up to the promotion

or your expectations

question

more conversation starters for couples

What is something humorous you recall about your first weeks or months of dating?

question

7

more conversation starters for couples

What was one of the
most inspiring funerals or
memorial services
you have ever attended?

Complete the following:

"I wish we could travel

to _____ and

have _____for

breakfast/lunch/dinner/dessert."

What is a common object you owned as a child—so common that you did not keep it but you wish you had because it is considered valuable today?

If you could own and operate your own business (and be guaranteed of its success), what would it be?

question

11

If you had to give up sight, hearing, the ability to speak, or the ability to walk, which would you choose? Which would you be most resistant to giving up?

question

12

more conversation starters for couples

If you could have four different homes and live in four different parts of the U.S. during the four seasons, state the location and season that you would live in these homes.

more conversation starters for couples

What famous person (living) would you like to meet?

Name one or two books,

other than the Bible,

that have significantly

influenced your thinking.

Usually "new" is presumed to also mean "improved." What is something you wish had not changed over the years?

If you had a magic wand

and could change anything

in your life right now,

what would you change?

One of life's great delights is surprising someone. Recall participating in a wonderful surprise by doing one or more of the following:

- Presenting a special gift
- Plotting and/or attending a surprise party
- Your unexpected appearance or phone call

question

18

more conversation starters for couples

If you could own a prop from a
favorite movie or television show,
what would be the prop?

(Some examples to spur your imagination:
Dorothy's red shoes from *The Wizard of Oz*,
a light saber from *Star Wars*, Barney Fife's pistol,
one of James Bond's cars, a lab coat from *ER*,
Moses' staff from *The Ten Commandments*,
the volleyball from *Cast Away*,
a basketball from *Hoosiers*)

If you could free

someone of a burden,

who would that be?

What are two things that

happened today, and

how did you feel about them?

question

21

Name someone with whom you have lost contact over the years and wonder how the person's doing.

Name something in your hometown that has been torn down and/or replaced, and describe how you feel about it being gone.

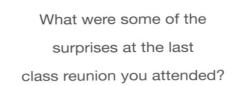

What were some of the
surprises at the last
class reunion you attended?

What is one of the most
difficult transitions you
have ever made?

more conversation starters for couples

If you knew that your very next prayer would be answered, what would you ask God for?

question

26

more conversation starters for couples

Name the person you know
who most personifies
perseverance.

While your partner is shopping across the street, you have an hour to browse in a large bookstore. In what two sections are you likely to spend most of your time?

☐ Fiction   ☐ Magazines   ☐ Religious/inspirational

☐ Children's books   ☐ Biography   ☐ Marriage/parenting

☐ Arts & crafts   ☐ Personal finance

☐ Psychology/self-help   ☐ Literature   ☐ Hobbies

☐ Career/management/ leadership

☐ Sports   ☐ Humor   ☐ other_____

question

28

more conversation starters for couples

Recall a time when you felt the actions of a person or group grossly misrepresented the true character and person of Christ.

Recall a time when adversity became a catalyst for spiritual growth.

question

30

more conversation starters for couples

If you could have any entertainer perform for your birthday, who would you choose?

question

31

Which person in
the Bible do you
most identify with?

What talent or skill do you
wish you possessed?

question

33

If you could demonstrate
patience in one area of life,
what would it be?

Jesus asked Peter, James, and John to accompany Him into the Garden of Gethsemane. Which three people would you ask to join you in praying during a crisis?

more conversation starters for couples

Name a well-known person that you've met. How did you feel in his or her presence?

Recall a favorite feature about the home you grew up in. Recall a favorite feature of the neighborhood.

What is something you would not change about your life right now?

A project that I'm

putting off is . . .

If your house was on fire and everyone (including pets) was safe outside, and you could safely retrieve one personal item (other than photo albums), what would you choose?

question
40

more conversation starters for couples

If you were imprisoned for your faith and could only have one book of the Bible with you to read, what would you choose?

If you could adopt one personality trait from someone you know, what would you take and from whom?

Congratulations! You have the winning bid in an auction for items once owned by famous people (living or deceased). Name the famous original item and the item for which you bid.

If you could have been the creator of any single piece of well-known art, music, or literature, which would you choose?

What is one of the most
significant sermons, messages,
or presentations you've ever heard?
What impact did it have on you?

Imagine that you discover you're related to someone famous. Who would you like it to be, knowing that the discovery would mean a new and ongoing relationship?

If you could find something in your attic that you thought was lost forever, what would it be?

With whom among your deceased relatives do you wish you could have been better acquainted?

Recall one of the best days
of your life, when you felt
especially alive and joyful.

Who is the best boss

you've ever had?

If you were suddenly gifted as a writer, describe the first book you'd publish.

Other than news of a death, what is the most disturbing personal news you've ever received?

Recall a time when
you were delighted or
surprised to be chosen.

How would you feel if you were to learn that you were moving to another city in a few months? What would you miss the least? What and who would you miss the most?

A "mulligan" is the second chance to hit a golf shot after flubbing the first shot. Complete this sentence: "Something in my life for which I wished I could have played a mulligan is . . ."

If you could be on the cover of any magazine, which one would it be, and what would be the caption or headline?

Charlie Brown never successfully kicked the football while Lucy was holding it for him. How about your "almosts"? Complete this sentence: "Sometimes I wonder if I will ever . . ."

question

57

more conversation starters for couples

For what sports event would you like to go back and reverse the outcome?

If you had access to any living person for advice, who would you call and concerning what?

more conversation starters for couples

For what special location (or occasion) would you like to have a special VIP pass? For example: the White House or Carnegie Hall (or the Olympics or Rose Bowl Parade)

What is the hardest

phone call you've

ever had to make?

Of the people you know, who seems most satisfied with his or her job? What would be your dream job?

What do you think
is the toughest decision
you ever made?

If you could give a substantial amount of money to someone in need right now, to whom would you give it?

What is your favorite

month of the year?

If you were a contestant on *Jeopardy!*, what would you hope would be one of the categories?

question

more conversation starters for couples

What do you think would be
the hardest thing about being
President of the United States?
What aspect of the job do you think
you would enjoy the most?

Jacob tricked his brother, Esau, and deceived his father, Isaac. Describe a time when you were tricked or lied to.

Recall a schoolboy/
schoolgirl crush.

What birthday or holiday would you like (or not like) to live over again?

Describe a time when you lost or broke something belonging to someone else.

Recall an encounter with a snake, mouse, spider, bee, toad, or any other creature that gives you the creeps.

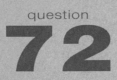

My first time on a stage that

I can remember was . . .

Can you recall a time when you
struggled with doubt concerning
one or more of the following:

God's existence

God's love

God's power

God's justice

God's wisdom

God's plan

God's timing

God's faithfulness

God's will

What would you like to
have season tickets to?

One of my disappointments

from last year was . . .

If you could discover
a cure for any disease,
what would it be?
(If you choose cancer,
try to be specific.)

Recall a movie whose ending you would like to rewrite. How would your version end?

If you could be fluent in

another language, which would

you choose and why?

Recall a practical joke played on you and/or recall one you played on someone else.

Create a new national holiday commemorating an historical event or person. What, why, and when?

David was tormented by an ungodly King Saul. Recall someone who had authority over you whom you found very difficult to respect.

If you could have the speaking voice of anyone you've heard, who would it be? If you could have the singing voice of anyone you've heard, who would it be?

Each of you flip a coin and answer
the appropriate question below:

HEADS : What was something encouraging
or positive that happened today?

TAILS : What was something disappointing
or difficult that happened today?

question
84

more conversation starters for couples

The Good Shepherd provides for, protects, and guides His sheep. Which of those three duties of the Shepherd is most meaningful and encouraging to you in your life right now?

Barnabas was an encourager and mentor to the apostle Paul in the years immediately following Paul's conversion. Recall someone who was a spiritual encourager or mentor to you for a season.

Which of the Seven Natural Wonders
of the World would you most like to see?
Why this one wonder?

☐ The Grand Canyon (Arizona)

☐ The Great Barrier Reef (Australia)

☐ Harbor of Rio de Janeiro (Brazil)

☐ The northern lights, or aurora borealis (Alaska)

☐ Mount Everest (Nepal/Tibet)

☐ Paricutin volcano (Mexico)

☐ Victoria Falls (Zimbabwe/Zambia)

If I were young again,

I'd spend more time . . .

Something I miss is . . .

more conversation starters for couples

If I had one year to live,

something I'd like to do is . . .

question

90

more conversation starters for couples

Peter said to Jesus, "We've fished all night and haven't caught anything." Is there any area of your life where you feel that hard work is not paying off?

Jesus' disciples were rowing the boat for several hours against a contrary wind. Frustration is defined as a response to a blocked goal. Is there any area where you feel a goal or plan is being blocked?

question

92

more conversation starters for couples

Peter was awestruck by his experience of seeing Moses, Elijah, and Jesus on the Mount of Transfiguration. Can you recall a spiritual experience that was so real and powerful that you did not want it to end?

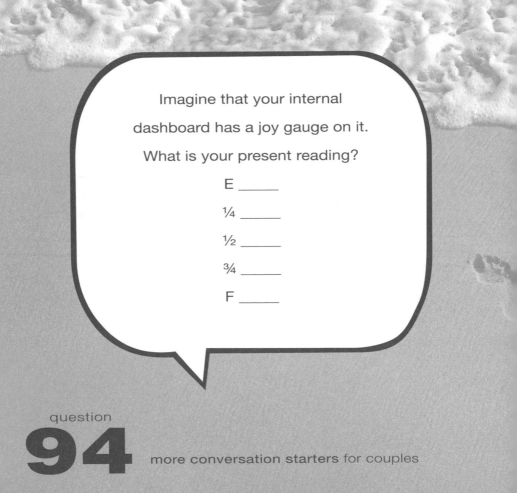

Imagine that your internal dashboard has a joy gauge on it. What is your present reading?

E _____

¼ _____

½ _____

¾ _____

F _____

question

94

more conversation starters for couples

Something about you that I hope never changes is . . .

Finish this sentence:

"I wish we'd had the camera

with us when . . ."

I think it would be wonderful to have

a hotel room in _____

and wake up the first morning and

throw open the curtains to behold

a magnificent view of

_____.

If you were to brag about me
to your friends, what
would you tell them?

You are the new owners of a six-bedroom bed-and-breakfast. Where is it located? What will be unique about it? What will you name it? Instead of numbering the rooms, innkeepers frequently give each room a name based on a theme. What will be your room theme? What will be the name of your favorite room?

question

Complete this sentence:

"It's too bad that kids today will

never know what it's like to . . ."

Take a few minutes to review the first one hundred items before answering this final one: From our sharing responses to these questions and statements, can you recall one of my answers that especially interested or surprised you?